ETIQUETTES OF TEACHERS AND STUDENTS

Authored by the Imām, the Mufassir,
'Abd al-Raḥmān bin Nāṣir As-Saʿdī

(MAY ALLĀH HAVE MERCY ON HIM)

Translated by Khālid Abū Zayd

lum'ah al lughah

© 2025 Lumʿah al-Lughah
@ LumahLughah • LumahLughah.com

Title: Etiquettes of Teachers and Students
Author: ʿAbd al-Raḥmān bin Nāṣir As-Saʿdī
Translator: Khālid Abū Zayd
Editing & Formatting: Dijam Studios

All rights reserved worldwide. No part of this book may be reprinted, reproduced or utilised in any form by any electronic, mechanical or other means, now known or hereafter invented, including photocopying and recording, without prior permission from the copyright holder.

TRANSLITERATION TABLE

CONSONANTS

ء ʾ	د d	ض ḍ	ك k
ب b	ذ dh	ط ṭ	ل l
ت t	ر r	ظ ḏh	م m
ث th	ز z	ع ʿ	ن n
ج j	س s	غ gh	هـ h
ح ḥ	ش sh	ف f	و w
خ kh	ص ṣ	ق q	ي y

VOWELS

SHORT	◌َ a	◌ِ i	◌ُ u
LONG	ـَا ā	ـِي ī	ـُو ū
DIPHTHONGS	ـَو aw	ـَي ay	

SALUTATIONS

ﷺ	May Allāh extol the name of the Prophet and protect him from any harm

عَلَيْهِ السَّلَامُ	Peace be upon him	رَضِيَ اللهُ عَنْهُ	Allāh be pleased with him

CONTENTS

Translators Preface..8

Publishers Introduction..10

A Brief Biography of the Author..........................14

ETIQUETTES OF TEACHERS AND STUDENTS

The Foundation of All Knowledge........................21

Prioritising What Benefits Most............................23

Teaching by Level of Comprehension..................24

The Teacher's Duty: Advice, Patience, & Care.....26

Honouring the Teacher...29

Correcting with Wisdom & Manners....................32

Humility in Returning to the Truth......................33

Saying 'Allāh Knows Best' when Uncertain..........34

Evidence-Based Discussion....................................36

Avoiding Fanaticism..37

Seeking Knowledge for Worldly Aims..................38

Acting Upon One's Knowledge..............................39

Beneficial Methods in Teaching and Learning....41

Repetition, Testing, and Revision..............................42

Good Conduct with Fellow Students....................43

Helping One Another in Learning........................44

Avoiding Obsession with Faults...............................45

Contentment and Simplicity......................................46

Spreading Beneficial Knowledge...............................47

Unity, Love, and Sincere Brotherhood....................48

ĀDĀB AL-MUʿALLIMĪN WAL-MUTAʿALLIMĪN

Ādāb al-Muʿallimīn wal-Mutaʿallimīn, arabic....53

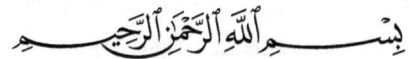

IN THE NAME OF ALLĀH, THE MOST
MERCIFUL, THE BESTOWER OF MERCY

TRANSLATORS PREFACE

In preparing this English edition of *Etiquettes of Teachers and Students*, I have sought to remain faithful to the words and intent of the noble author, Shaykh ʿAbd al-Raḥmān al-Nāṣir al-Saʿdī (رحمه الله), while presenting it in a clear and accessible style for contemporary readers. The Shaykh's Arabic is concise, flowing, and full of meaning. Rendering this into English required careful attention so that none of its clarity or weight was lost.

Where the original text contained long, interconnected sentences — characteristic of classical Arabic writing — I have, when necessary, divided them into shorter sentences to preserve readability in English. Likewise, sub-headings have been added throughout to make each principle or etiquette stand out clearly, reflecting the way the Shaykh arranged his thoughts and aiding the reader in following the progression of the work.

On occasion, brief explanatory words have been inserted in brackets. These are not commentaries, but light clarifications intended only to make implicit meanings more explicit for readers without altering the author's intent.

My aim has been to strike a balance: to retain the distinctive rhythm and dignity of the Arabic, while producing a polished English text that reads smoothly and benefits both teachers and students. It is my prayer that this translation serves as a means by which non-Arabic speakers may taste the wisdom and sincerity that permeate the writings of Shaykh al-Saʿdī, and that it encourages all seekers of knowledge to embody the manners and etiquettes set down here.

May Allāh accept this work, overlook its shortcomings, and make it a source of benefit in this life and the Hereafter.

PUBLISHERS INTRODUCTION

All praise is due to Allāh, the Lord of all creation. We praise Him, seek His help, and ask His forgiveness. We seek refuge in Him from the evils of our own souls and from our misdeeds. Whomsoever Allāh guides, none can misguide; and whomsoever He leaves to stray, none can guide.

I bear witness that there is no deity worthy of worship but Allāh alone, having no partner, and I bear witness that Muḥammad is His servant and Messenger — may Allāh's peace and blessings be upon him, his family, and his Companions, and upon those who follow them in goodness until the Day of Judgement.

To Proceed: The pursuit of knowledge is among the greatest of obligations, and its fruits are among the noblest of fruits. Through it the servant knows his Lord, rectifies his religion, and attains everlasting felicity. Knowledge is the path that leads to Paradise, and the scholars are the inheritors of the Prophets.

Yet knowledge cannot be attained by negligence, nor can it bear its fruits without sincerity, patience, humility, and good manners.

One who learns without manners is like a farmer sowing seeds in barren land — he toils but reaps nothing.

This treatise, *Etiquettes of Teachers and Students*, authored by the noble scholar Shaykh ʿAbd al-Raḥmān bin Nāṣir al-Saʿdī (رَحِمَهُ ٱللَّهُ), is a concise but comprehensive reminder of the etiquettes and obligations that safeguard the path of learning and teaching. The author was known for his clarity, wisdom, and balanced style; and in these pages, he sets down principles which, if embodied, preserve the beauty of knowledge and protect it from corruption.

He begins with the foundation of sincerity — making every step in seeking and conveying knowledge an act of worship intended for the Face of Allāh. He then outlines the method of prioritising what is most important in learning, presenting knowledge gradually and in proportion, and showing patience towards students. He stresses the rights of teachers and students, the dangers of arrogance, fanaticism, and corrupt intentions, and the necessity of embodying knowledge through action.

He concludes with the vital importance of unity, brotherhood, and the avoidance of division — principles that are as urgent today as they were in the time of the early generations.

The value of this work is not limited to teachers or students in formal institutions; rather, it is a guide for every Muslim engaged in the pursuit of knowledge, whether great or small. It reminds us that knowledge is not mere information, but a trust, a light, and a path leading to the pleasure of Allāh. Without sincerity and manners, knowledge becomes a burden rather than a blessing. With them, knowledge flourishes, benefits the individual, and spreads goodness to society.

We live in a time of great distractions and conflicting voices, where access to information is abundant but the light of true knowledge is rare. It is therefore more necessary than ever that seekers of knowledge begin with purification of the heart, respect for teachers, humility before the truth, and cooperation upon righteousness. Within these qualities lies the secret of success — for the individual student, and for the community of believers at large.

May Allāh make this work a means of benefit, guidance, and light for teachers, students, and all seekers of knowledge. May He reward the author for his service to Islām and its people, and may He grant us sincerity in speech and action. Indeed, He is al-Wahhāb (the Bestower).

A BRIEF BIOGRAPHY OF THE AUTHOR

He is the Imām, the Mufassir, the great scholar, Abū 'Abd Allāh 'Abd al-Raḥmān bin Nāṣir bin 'Abd Allāh bin Nāṣir Āl Sa'dī, from the tribe of Tamīm.

He was born in the town of 'Unayzah in the region al-Qaṣīm, on the 12th of Muḥarram in the year 1307H.

His mother passed away when he was four years old, and his father when he was seven. Thus, he grew up an orphan; yet, he was raised well and nurtured upon goodness.

From his early childhood, his intelligence and strong desire for knowledge drew attention. After the passing of his father, he began to read the Qur'ān, and he memorised it completely by heart, mastering its recitation at the age of eleven. He then devoted himself to seeking knowledge from the scholars of his town, and from scholars who visited it. He strove diligently until he attained a large portion of every branch of knowledge.

When he reached the age of twenty-three, he began teaching, combining both learning and teaching, devoting all his time to that. By the year 1350 AH, teaching in his town had become centred upon him, and all the students relied upon him for their studies.

SOME OF HIS TEACHERS

- Shaykh Ibrāhīm bin Ḥamd bin Jāssir,
- Shaykh Muḥammad bin ʿAbd al-Karīm al-Shibl,
- Shaykh Ṣāliḥ bin ʿUthmān al-Qāḍī,
- Shaykh ʿAbd Allāh bin ʿĀyiḍ,
- Shaykh Saʿb al-Quwayjirī,
- Shaykh ʿAlī al-Sanānī,
- Shaykh ʿAlī al-Nāṣir Abū Wādī,
- Shaykh Muḥammad bin ʿAbd al-ʿAzīz al-Māniʿ,
- Shaykh Muḥammad al-Shinqīṭī.

SOME OF HIS STUDENTS

- Shaykh ʿAbd Allāh bin al-Bassām,
- Shaykh Muḥammad al-Amīn al-Shanqīṭī,
- Shaykh Ṣāliḥ Āl al-Shaykh al-Saʿdī,
- Shaykh Muḥammad bin ʿAqīl,
- Shaykh Ṣāliḥ al-Bulayhī,
- Shaykh Muḥammad Ṣāliḥ al-ʿUthaymīn.

A GLIMPSE OF HIS CHARACTER

The Shaykh possessed lofty manners and noble qualities. He was humble with young and old, rich and poor alike. He would spend part of his time in gatherings for those who wished to attend, which would turn into academic assemblies. These sessions included scholarly and social discussions that brought immense benefit to those present, transforming ordinary sittings into acts of worship and circles of knowledge.

He would speak to each person according to what suited them, discussing beneficial matters for both their worldly and religious affairs. He often resolved disputes with just reconciliation that satisfied both parties. He was compassionate towards the poor, needy, and strangers, offering assistance within his means and encouraging others known for their generosity to do likewise.

He was marked by refined conduct, chastity, honesty, and firmness in all his affairs. He was among the best of people in teaching and in making knowledge easily understood, organising lessons with precision, and holding debates between his advanced students to sharpen their minds. He would even give prizes to those who memorised certain texts, ensuring that no one was deprived of encouragement.

He consulted his students in selecting the most beneficial books for study, leaning towards what the majority desired, and in case of equal division, he would decide. His students never tired of his long lessons, for they delighted in his company. Hence, he had a great number of accomplished students, and his influence continues. May Allāh bless his life and ours, and grant us and him the provision of righteous deeds.

HIS STANDING IN KNOWLEDGE

He had comprehensive knowledge of fiqh, both its uṣūl and furūʿ. In his early years, he adhered closely to the Ḥanbalī madhhab, following his teachers, and even authored a poem of about four hundred lines in fiqh with a brief commentary. However, he later chose not to circulate it, as it reflected his early views

His greatest benefit came from the works of Shaykh al-Islām Ibn Taymiyyah and his student Ibn al-Qayyim, from which he gained immense light and clarity in uṣūl, tawḥīd, tafsīr, fiqh, and other beneficial sciences. This led him to no longer confine himself strictly to the

Ḥanbalī school; rather, he would adopt what was supported by evidence from the Sharī'ah, while never disparaging the scholars of the madhāhib as some zealots do.

He excelled particularly in tafsīr, having read many works and becoming distinguished in it. He authored a great tafsīr of the Qur'ān in several volumes. He would regularly read and explain the Qur'ān with his students directly, deriving profound meanings and insights that captivated listeners with his eloquence, fluency, and mastery in presenting evidences and narratives. Whoever met him, read to him, or engaged in discussion with him recognised his vast knowledge. Likewise, whoever reads his writings and fatāwā comes to know his rank in scholarship.

HIS WRITINGS

Among his works are:

- Tafsīr al-Qur'ān al-Karīm, entitled Taysīr al-Karīm al-Mannān,
- Ḥāshiyah on al-Iqna',
- Al-Durrah al-Mukhtaṣarah fī Maḥāsin al-Islām,
- Al-Khuṭab al-'Aṣriyyah al-Qayyimah,

- Al-Qawāʿid al-Ḥisān li-Tafsīr al-Qurʾān,
- Tanzīh al-Dīn wa-Ḥamalatihi wa-Rijālihi,
- Al-Ḥaqq al-Wāḍiḥ al-Mubīn,
- Tawḍīḥ al-Kāfiyah al-Shāfiyah,
- Wujūb al-Taʿāwun bayna al-Muslimīn,
- Al-Qawl al-Sadīd fī Maqāṣid al-Tawḥīd,
- Mukhtaṣar fī Uṣūl al-Fiqh,
- Taysīr al-Laṭīf al-Mannān fī Khulāṣat Tafsīr al-Qurʾān,
- Al-Riyāḍ al-Nāḍirah.

In addition, he had numerous scattered notes, many fatāwā in response to questions from near and far, and annotations on many works. Writing came easily to him, and he produced a great deal of scholarly material.

HIS AIM IN WRITING

His sole aim in authorship was the spread of knowledge and the call to truth. For that reason, he authored, wrote, and printed whatever he was able to from his works, seeking no worldly gain. Rather, he would distribute them freely so that benefit might be widespread. May Allāh reward him on behalf of Islām and the Muslims with the best of rewards, and grant us and him that which earns His pleasure.

HIS PASSING

After a blessed life of nearly sixty-nine years in the service of knowledge, he returned to his Lord in the year 1376H (1957 CE), in the city of 'Unayzah. May Allāh have abundant mercy upon him.

ETIQUETTES OF TEACHERS AND STUDENTS

IMAM ABD AL-RAHMAN AL-SA'DI

①

THE FOUNDATION OF ALL KNOWLEDGE: SINCERITY AND SEEKING NEARNESS TO ALLĀH

It is incumbent upon the people of knowledge, both teachers and students, to make sincerity and seeking closeness to Allāh the foundation of their affair, upon which they build all their actions, whether active or at rest — which is the most noble, complete, beneficial, and comprehensive of the acts of worship.

And they should constantly examine this noble foundation in every small and great matter of theirs.

So, if they study or review, research or debate, convey or listen, write or memorise, revise their own lessons, review them or other books alongside them, sit in a gathering of knowledge, walk to attend gatherings of knowledge, purchase books or anything that aids in acquiring knowledge, then sincerity to Allāh and seeking His recompense and His reward must accompany them. So that their entire engagement becomes an act of drawing close, of obedience, and a journey towards Allāh and His generosity.

And so, they actualise his saying (ﷺ): *"Whoever treads a path seeking knowledge, Allāh will make easy for him thereby a path to Paradise."*[1]

So, every path, whether tangible or intangible, trodden by the people of knowledge which aids in knowledge or acquiring it, is included in this.

---

1 Ṣaḥīḥ Muslim (no. 2699).

②
THE METHOD OF LEARNING: PRIORITISING WHAT IS MOST IMPORTANT AND MOST BENEFICIAL

Then after this, it becomes necessary to begin with the most important, then the next most important of the religious sciences and what aids that from the Arabic sciences, and the details of this are well-known. And he should take the easiest path that leads to his intended goal and choose from the works of the field he engages in, the best, clearest, and most beneficial of them.

And if able, make his overwhelming concern and effort the memorisation of that book, or by studying it repetitively such that its meanings are understood and retained by him; then he should continue to review and repeat what he has already covered.

③

TEACHING ACCORDING TO THE STUDENT'S LEVEL OF COMPREHENSION

And it is upon the teacher to consider the mental capacity of the student and the strength or weakness of his comprehension and not let him engage with a book that does not suit his level; doing otherwise would fall short of sincere guidance, for the little that he understands and grasps is better than the large portion that is liable to being misunderstood and forgotten.

Likewise, he should present to him the clarification and explanation of what is being studied as much as the student's understanding can grasp, and he should not mix one issue with another, nor move from one type of issue to another until he comprehends and actualises what has previously been studied, for that secures the earlier point and frees his understanding for what follows.

But if he introduces the topics in a confused heap, intermingling them before the student has understood each one properly, then this is a cause for what was learnt first to be lost and what is to be studied after to be misunderstood, and then the unresolved issues crowd upon him, so he becomes weary of them and his inclination to returning back to review them diminishes.

So, this matter must not be neglected.

THE TEACHER'S DUTY OF SINCERE ADVISING, EXERCISING PATIENCE, AND NURTURING THE STUDENT

The teacher must advise the student in every way he can through teaching, and show patience at his lack of understanding, poor manners, and harshness, whilst being keen to correct him and improve his conduct. This is because the student has a right over the teacher, by him seeking knowledge that benefits him and others, by choosing that teacher specifically rather than others and because what he carries of knowledge is the very commodity of the teacher, which he preserves, develops, and seeks profitable gains with.

So, he is a true child of the teacher and his inheritor. He, the Most High, said [upon the tongue of Zakarīyyah (عَلَيْهِ ٱلسَّلَامُ)]:

﴿فَهَبْ لِى مِن لَّدُنكَ وَلِيًّا ۝ يَرِثُنِى وَيَرِثُ مِنْ ءَالِ يَعْقُوبَ﴾

"Grant me from Yourself an heir. Who will inherit me and inherit from the family of Yaʿqūb."[2]

---

2   Sūrah Maryam: 5-6.

What is meant here is the inheritance of knowledge and wisdom.

So, the teacher is rewarded and recompensed for his teaching, whether the student understands or not.

But if the student understands what he was taught, and benefits himself and others, then the reward flows continuously to the teacher as long as the benefit remains continuous and unbroken — and this is a trade in which the successful compete.

Therefore, the teacher must strive earnestly to establish and grow this trade, for it consists of his deeds and the effects of his deeds.

He, the Most High, said:

﴿ إِنَّا نَحْنُ نُحْيِ ٱلْمَوْتَىٰ وَنَكْتُبُ مَا قَدَّمُوا۟ وَءَاثَـٰرَهُمْ وَكُلَّ شَىْءٍ أَحْصَيْنَـٰهُ فِىٓ إِمَامٍ مُّبِينٍ ۝ ﴾

"Indeed, it is We who bring the dead to life and record what they sent before them and the traces they left behind."[3]

---

3 Sūrah Yā-Sīn: 12.

'*What they sent before them*' refers to the deeds they directly performed, and '*the traces they left behind*' refer to what resulted from their actions, be it benefits, advantages, or the opposite thereof.

And he should encourage the student by every means and not to make him grow weary by occupying him with whatever makes difficult his understanding of the various sciences and their components.

⑤
THE STUDENT'S OBLIGATION TO HONOUR HIS TEACHER

The student must respect his teacher and show good manners towards him as much as he is able, because of the general and specific right the teacher has over him.

As for the general right: the teacher of good has prepared himself to benefit the people through his teaching and religious questions, so his right upon the people is like the right of all those who do good, and there is no kindness greater or more beneficial than that of one who guides the people in the matters of their religion, teaches them what they are ignorant of, and alerts them to what they have neglected.

And as a result of that, goodness is achieved, harm is removed, the religion is spread, and beneficial knowledge is disseminated, which is the most beneficial thing for those alive and those who come after them from their descendants and others.

Were it not for knowledge, people would be like cattle, stumbling about in darkness, blindly wandering in their misguidance. It is the light by which one is guided through the darkness, and it is the life of hearts, souls, religion, and the world.

And a land in which there is no one to clarify to the people the matters of their religion, and guide them concerning what befalls them regarding the affairs of what they are in need of, there is no good in living there.

So, the one whose kindness and influence are of this nature — how could it not be incumbent upon every Muslim to love him, respect him, and fulfil his rights?

As for his specific right over the student, it is because of what he has given in teaching, and his care in guiding him and raising him to the highest ranks.

The benefit gained from fathers and mothers is not equal to the benefit gained from teachers, who nurture people with the small aspects of knowledge before the great ones, who spend the best of their time and the finest of their contemplation, to explain to the seekers of guidance through every way and means they can.

If someone does good to a person with a monetary gift, which benefits him but then perishes and vanishes, he still owes a great right to the benefactor — then what about the numerous, diverse, and beneficial gifts of knowledge, whose benefit remains as long as the servant lives and after his death, and continues in proportion to the nature of those gifts?

At that point, he recognises his right, respects him, and shows good manners to him, not going against his direction and guidance. And he should sit before him with proper manners, showing the utmost need for his knowledge, supplicating for him in his presence and absence, and if the teacher grants him a benefit or clarification of knowledge, he should not show that he already knew it before that.

Even if he already knows it, he should still listen attentively like one eagerly seeking benefit.

This is regarding what he knows — so what then of what he does not know?

For this reason, this etiquette is commendable with everyone, in matters of knowledge and in conversations on religious and worldly affairs.

6

CORRECTING THE TEACHER: WITH GENTLENESS, WISDOM, AND GOOD MANNERS

If the teacher makes a mistake in something, he should be corrected gently and kindly, according to the situation, and he should not say to him: "You are wrong" or "It is not as you say." Rather, he should use gentle wording, so the teacher realises his mistake without his heart becoming unsettled. For indeed, this is from the necessary rights and more conducive to arriving at what is correct.

Certainly, a refutation that comes with bad manners and causes the heart to become uneasy, prevents one from understanding and pursuing what is correct.

⑦
THE TEACHER'S HUMILITY IN RETURNING TO THE TRUTH

And just as this is required of the student; the teacher, if he errs, must also return to the truth.

What he already said should not prevent him, if he later sees the truth contrary to it, from reviewing and returning to the truth. For indeed, this is a sign of ones being just and having humility before the truth; therefore, it is obligatory to follow what is correct, whether it comes from the young or the old.

And from the blessings of Allāh upon the teacher is that he finds among his students one who alerts him to his mistake, guiding him to what is correct, thus removing his being continuous upon ignorance.

This requires gratitude to Allāh, and then gratitude to the one through whom Allāh brought guidance, whether it be a student or other than him.

⑧
THE TEACHERS SAYING 'ALLĀH KNOWS BEST' WHEN UNCERTAIN

And from the greatest duties upon teachers in regards to what they do not know, is for them to say: "Allāh knows best," and this does not diminish their status; rather, it is from that which increases their status, and indicates their following the religion and their pursuit for what is correct.

There contains many a benefit found within (the teacher) withholding himself from what he does not know:

From them: that this is obligatory upon him.

And from them: that if he refrains and says: "I do not know," then how swiftly knowledge of it comes to him; either through his own review or the review of another. For indeed, when the student sees his teacher refrain, he strives and exerts himself to acquire knowledge of it and to present it to the teacher — how excellent is this outcome!

And from them: that if he refrains from what he does not know, it is an indication of his trustworthiness and precision in what he asserts of matters, just as one who is known to be bold in speaking about what he does not know, that becomes a cause for doubt in everything he says, even in the clear matters.

And from them: that when the students see from him his refraining from that which he does not know, this serves as a lesson for them and guidance to this virtuous practice, and emulating conduct and actions is more effective than merely emulating words.

⑨
ENCOURAGING EVIDENCE-BASED DISCUSSION

And from that which aids in achieving this goal is that the teacher opens for the students the door of discussing the issues and presenting evidence regarding them, and that the intent be one, namely: following that which the proof and evidence deem strongest.

For when he keeps this aim at the forefront of his eyes and theirs, minds are enlightened, the points of evidence and proofs become known, truths are followed, and the original aim, along with its fruits of knowing the truth and following it, are realised.

AVOIDING FANATICISM FOR OPINIONS AND INDIVIDUALS

And let him be warned (and again) let him be warned from fanaticism of opinions and their proponents, which is to make the aim of debate merely to defend the opinion he himself uttered or that of someone he reveres.

For indeed, fanaticism undermines sincerity, strips knowledge of its splendour, obscures realities, and opens the doors to dispute and rancour.

In contrast, fairness is the adornment of knowledge, and the hallmark of sincerity, goodwill, and success.

THE PROHIBITION OF SEEKING KNOWLEDGE FOR WORLDLY AIMS

And let him be warned of seeking knowledge for corrupt purposes and evil intentions; such as boasting, disputation, showing off, seeking to be heard of, or using it as a means to worldly ambitions and leadership.

Such is not the condition of the people of knowledge who are truly its people.

And whoever seeks knowledge and uses it for his evil purposes or for showing off, he shall have no share in the Hereafter.

① ②
ACTING UPON ONE'S KNOWLEDGE

And among the greatest duties upon the people of knowledge is that they embody what knowledge calls to in terms of noble character, righteous deeds, and teaching.

They are the most worthy of adorning themselves with beautiful manners and relinquishing every lowly trait, and they are the most worthy of fulfilling both outward and inward obligations and of abstaining from prohibitions, due to the knowledge and understanding with which they have been distinguished, which others have not attained, and because they are the examples to whom people follow in their affairs, and because the criticisms and objections directed at them — when they abandon what knowledge calls to — are greater than those directed at others.

And likewise, the Salaf (righteous predecessors) would use actions as an aid for the strengthening of their knowledge; for if they acted upon it, it became firmly established, endured, flourished, and its blessings increased.

But if they abandoned acting upon it, it would depart, or its blessings would vanish.

For the spirit, life, and essence of knowledge lies in upholding it through practice, conduct, teaching, and sincere counsel. And there is no power nor strength except with Allāh.

①③
FOLLOWING A BENEFICIAL METHOD IN TEACHING AND LEARNING

It is necessary to follow a beneficial method when examining a topic in learning and teaching. When the teacher begins addressing an issue, he should clarify it and convey it, ensuring it reaches the understanding of the students by every means at his disposal, through precise expression, giving examples, illustration, and careful explanation.

Then he should not move on from it to another issue until it has been firmly established and understood by the students.

Nor should he allow the students to move on from a topic that has not yet been fully established to another topic, until they have mastered and comprehended it.

For indeed, moving from one topic to another before completing it confuses the mind, deprives of benefit, and muddles the issues one with one another.

THE ROLE OF REPETITION, TESTING, AND REVISION

It is also necessary to keep up with the students' memorised material and their knowledge by means of repetition and testing, and urging them to revise and consolidate their knowledge, and to repeat the lesson.

For indeed, learning is like planting trees, while study, revision, and repetition are like watering them and removing harmful elements, so that they may grow and increase continually.

GOOD CONDUCT WITH FELLOW STUDENTS

Just as the student is required to show reverence and proper conduct towards his teacher, so too must he show respect and good manners toward his fellow students who learn alongside him, and upon him is to show them respect and honour.

For companionship in seeking knowledge encompasses many rights. They have the right of brotherhood and companionship, the right of respect for their engagement in that which benefits themselves and others, which is their affiliation to their teacher, because they are in the station of his own children, and they have the right of benefiting one another.

①⑥
HELPING ONE ANOTHER IN LEARNING

For this reason, one ought not to neglect any possible means within his ability to benefit those whom he is able to benefit, by way of teaching them what they are ignorant of, engaging in discussion with them in mutual cooperation upon goodness, and guiding them to that which benefits them.

Their gatherings at all times should be an opportunity rich in benefit: the one who is deficient learns from the one above him, the knowledgeable teaches the one who is not, and they exchange and discuss beneficial issues.

①⑦
AVOIDING OBSESSION WITH THE FAULTS OF OTHERS

And they should limit their concern to that which they are currently busy with, and beware of occupying themselves with others, probing into their conditions, and finding fault with them, for that is engagement in sin.

And a sin committed by the people of knowledge is graver than that of others, because the evidence against them is stronger, and due to others following them in their example, and because those whose nature inclines to evil among others take them as a justification for themselves.

And preoccupation with others wastes beneficial interests and precious time and deprives knowledge of its splendour and light.

① ⑧

CONTENTMENT AND SIMPLICITY IN THE PATH OF KNOWLEDGE

Know that contentment with little provision and simplicity in livelihood are required of everyone, especially those engaged in the pursuit of knowledge, for it is as though it is incumbent upon them.

This is because knowledge is the task of one's entire life, or most of it; so whenever worldly occupations and necessities compete with it, deficiency ensues.

And simplicity and contentment are among the greatest means of curbing worldly distractions and enabling the student to devote himself to what he is engaged in.

SINCERE ADVICE AND SPREADING BENEFICIAL KNOWLEDGE

Among the etiquettes of the scholar and the student is to offer sincere advice and to disseminate beneficial knowledge to the utmost extent possible.

Even if a person learns a single issue and imparts it, that is from the blessing of knowledge.

And due to the fruits of knowledge being that people take it from you, then whoever is miserly with his knowledge, his knowledge dies with him.

He may forget it whilst he is alive, just as him disseminating his knowledge is a second life for him, and a preservation of his knowledge, and Allāh rewards him in accordance with his deeds.

⓶⓪

UNITY, LOVE, AND SINCERE BROTHERHOOD AMONG THE PEOPLE OF KNOWLEDGE

Among the most important duties is to strive to bring their ranks together and to bring hearts into harmony upon that, and to eliminate the causes of malice, enmity, and hatred among themselves.

They should make this matter the focus of their attention and the goal towards which they strive by every means, for the objective is one, the aim is one, and the benefit is shared.

They realise this affair by loving everyone who belongs to the people of knowledge, or who has a contribution therein, or is engaged in it, or brings benefit.

They do not allow corrupt motives to take hold of them and prevent them from attaining this noble aim.

Thus, they love one another, defend one another, and offer advice to anyone they see turning away from one another, and they demonstrate that insignificant matters which invite to the opposite of love and harmony, should never be placed in front of the fundamental comprehensive principles which brings about unity of word.

They should not allow the enemies of knowledge, whether from among the laymen or others, to gain the opportunity to corrupt their relationships and divide their word.

For realising this noble objective and upholding it are from the benefits and advantages which are innumerable, even if it contained nothing other than the fact that this is the very religion which the Legislator has urged through every means.

Those most obliged to uphold this are its true people, for it is among the greatest proofs of genuine counsel and sincerity, which are both the foundation and spirit of the religion.

Indeed, through this quality the slave is described as being truly from the people of knowledge, who are its people, about whom there has come in the Book and the Sunnah their praise and commendation, the mention of which is beyond the scope of this discussion.

It brings about an increase of knowledge, broader access to it, and diversity in its paths, all of which are evident.

When the people of knowledge follow a single way, it becomes possible for them to learn from one another and to teach one another.

But if each group among them isolates itself from the others and turns away from them, the benefit is cut off and replaced by its opposite, from: sectarianism, hatred, and probing the faults and errors of the other group.

All of this is contrary to both religion and reason, to what is required of the people of knowledge, and to what the righteous predecessors were upon. You will find that the one granted success is one who is sincere to Allāh in affirming His oneness and fulfilling His worship, both outwardly and inwardly, with sincerity and seeking reward, perfecting it to the extent of his ability.

He is sincere to the Book of Allāh by believing in all that it contains, devoting himself to learning it and the sciences related and subsidiary to it.

He is sincere to His Messenger (ﷺ) by believing in everything he brought, from both the fundamentals and the branches of the religion, giving precedence to love of him over every other love, after the love of Allāh (the Most High), and actualising his example in the external and internal aspects of the religion.

He is sincere to the leaders of the Muslims, their rulers, their scholars and their heads, loving good for them, striving to support them in it, by word and deed, loving that the people remain united in obedience to them and avoiding harmful opposition to them.

He is sincere to the general populace of the Muslims, loving for them what he loves for himself and hating for them what he hates for himself.

His outward actions confirm his inward state, his words are in accordance with his deeds, and he calls to this well-established principle and straight path.

So, we ask Allāh, the Most Generous, to grant us His love, and the love of those who love Him, and the love of deeds that bring us nearer to His love, and to bestow upon us mercy from Him; for indeed, He is al-Wahhāb (the Bestower).

And may Allāh extol and send blessings and peace upon Muḥammad, and upon his family and Companions.⁴

---

4 This was stated and written by the servant in need of his Lord, 'Abd al-Raḥmān al-Nāṣir bin Sa'dī (رحمه الله).

And it was copied from the author's handwriting by the servant in need of his Patron Lord, Muḥammad bin Sulaymān bin 'Abd al-'Azīz Āl Bassām.

Dated: 1st Dhū al-Ḥijjah 1412H

آداب المعلمين والمتعلمين للإمام السعدي

مِنْ عُلُومِ الشَّرِيعَةِ كُلِّهَا، نَاصِحًا لِرَسُولِهِ بِالإِيمَانِ بِكُلِّ مَا جَاءَ بِهِ مِنْ أُصُولِ الدِّينِ وَفُرُوعِهِ وَتَقْدِيمِ مَحَبَّتِهِ عَلَى كُلِّ مَحَبَّةٍ بَعْدَ مَحَبَّةِ اللهِ تَعَالَى، وَتَحْقِيقِ مُتَابَعَتِهِ فِي شَرَائِعِ الدِّينِ الظَّاهِرَةِ وَالبَاطِنَةِ، نَاصِحًا لِأَئِمَّةِ المُسْلِمِينَ؛ مِنْ وُلَاتِهِمْ وَعُلَمَائِهِمْ وَرُؤَسَائِهِمْ فِي مَحَبَّةِ الخَيْرِ لَهُمْ وَالسَّعْيِ فِي إِعَانَتِهِمْ عَلَيْهِ قَوْلًا وَفِعْلًا، وَمَحَبَّةِ اجْتِمَاعِ الرَّعِيَّةِ عَلَى طَاعَتِهِمْ وَعَدَمِ مُخَالَفَتِهِمُ الضَّارَّةِ، نَاصِحًا لِعَامَّةِ المُسْلِمِينَ، يُحِبُّ لَهُمْ مَا يُحِبُّ لِنَفْسِهِ وَيَكْرَهُ لَهُمْ مَا يَكْرَهُ لِنَفْسِهِ، وَيُصَدِّقُ ظَاهِرَهُ بَاطِنَهُ، وَأَقْوَالَهُ وَأَفْعَالَهُ، وَيَدْعُو إِلَى هَذَا الأَصْلِ القَوِيمِ وَالصِّرَاطِ المُسْتَقِيمِ.

فَنَسْأَلُ اللَّهَ الكَرِيمَ أَنْ يَرْزُقَنَا حُبَّهُ وَحُبَّ مَنْ يُحِبُّهُ، وَحُبَّ العَمَلِ الَّذِي يُقَرِّبُنَا إِلَى حُبِّهِ، وَيَهَبَ لَنَا مِنْ لَدُنْهُ رَحْمَةً إِنَّهُ هُوَ الوَهَّابُ.

وَصَلَّى اللهُ عَلَى مُحَمَّدٍ وَعَلَى آلِهِ وَصَحْبِهِ وَسَلَّمَ.

آداب المعلمين والمتعلمين للإمام السعدي

يَتَّصِفُ العَبْدُ بِأَنَّهُ مِنْ أَهْلِ العِلْمِ الَّذِينَ هُمْ أَهْلُهُ الَّذِينَ وَرَدَ فِي الكِتَابِ وَالسُّنَّةِ مِنْ مَدْحِهِمْ وَالثَّنَاءِ عَلَيْهِمْ مَا لَا يَتَّسِعُ هَذَا المَوْضِعُ لِذِكْرِهِ.

وَفِيهِ مِنْ تَكْثِيرِ العِلْمِ وَتَوْسِعَةِ الوُصُولِ إِلَيْهِ وَتَنَوُّعِ طُرُقِهِ مَا هُوَ مُشَاهَدٌ، فَإِنَّ أَهْلَ العِلْمِ إِذَا كَانَتْ طَرِيقَتُهُمْ وَاحِدَةً تَمَكَّنَ أَنْ يَتَعَلَّمَ بَعْضُهُمْ مِنْ بَعْضٍ، وَيُعَلِّمَ بَعْضُهُمْ بَعْضًا، وَإِذَا كَانَتْ كُلُّ طَائِفَةٍ مِنْهُمْ مُنْزَوِيَةً عَنِ الأُخْرَى مُنْحَرِفَةً عَنْهَا انْقَطَعَتِ الفَائِدَةُ وَحَلَّ مَحَلَّهَا ضِدُّهَا، وَحَصَلَ التَّعَصُّبُ وَالبُغْضُ وَالتَّفْتِيشُ عَنْ عُيُوبِ الطَّائِفَةِ الأُخْرَى وَأَغْلَاطِهَا، وَكُلُّ هَذَا مُنَافٍ لِلدِّينِ وَالعَقْلِ، وَلِمَا يَتَعَيَّنُ عَلَى أَهْلِ العِلْمِ، وَلِمَا كَانَ عَلَيْهِ السَّلَفُ الصَّالِحُ.

فَالمُوَفَّقُ تَجِدُهُ نَاصِحًا للهِ بِتَوْحِيدِهِ وَالقِيَامِ بِعُبُودِيَتِهِ ظَاهِرًا وَبَاطِنًا، بِإِخْلَاصٍ وَاحْتِسَابٍ وَتَكْمِيلٍ لَهَا بِحَسَبِ وُسْعِهِ، نَاصِحًا لِكِتَابِ اللهِ بِالإِيمَانِ بِمَا اشْتَمَلَ عَلَيْهِ، وَالإِقْبَالِ عَلَى تَعَلُّمِهِ وَتَعَلُّمِ مَا يَتَعَلَّقُ بِهِ وَيَتَفَرَّعُ عَنْهُ

وَغَايَةً يَسْعَوْنَ إِلَيْهَا بِكُلِّ طَرِيقٍ؛ لِأَنَّ المَطْلُوبَ وَاحِدٌ وَالقَصْدَ وَاحِدٌ، وَالمَصْلَحَةَ مُشْتَرَكَةٌ، فَيُحَقِّقُونَ هَذَا الأَمْرَ بِمَحَبَّةِ كُلِّ مَنْ كَانَ مِنْ أَهْلِ العِلْمِ وَمَنْ لَهُ قَدَمٌ فِيهِ أَوِ اشْتِغَالٌ أَوْ نَفْعٌ، وَلَا يَدَعُونَ الأَغْرَاضَ الفَاسِدَةَ تَمَلَّكُهُمْ وَتَمْنَعُهُمْ مِنْ هَذَا المَطْلُوبِ الجَلِيلِ، فَيُحِبُّ بَعْضُهُمْ بَعْضاً، وَيَذُبُّ بَعْضُهُمْ عَنْ بَعْضٍ، وَيَبْذُلُونَ النَّصِيحَةَ لِمَنْ رَأَوْهُ مُنْحَرِفًا عَنِ الآخَرِ، وَيُبَرْهِنُونَ عَلَى أَنَّ الأُمُورَ الجُزْئِيَّةَ الَّتِي تَدْعُو إِلَى ضِدِّ المَحَبَّةِ وَالإِئْتِلَافِ لَا تُقَدَّمُ عَلَى الأُصُولِ الكُلِّيَّةِ الَّتِي فِيهَا جَمْعُ الكَلِمَةِ.

وَلَا يَدَعُونَ أَعْدَاءَ العِلْمِ مِنَ العَوَامِ وَغَيْرِهِمْ يَتَمَكَّنُونَ مِنْ إِفْسَادِ ذَاتِ بَيْنِهِمْ وَتَفْرِيقِ كَلِمَتِهِمْ، فَإِنَّ فِي تَحْقِيقِ هَذَا المَقْصِدِ الجَلِيلِ وَالقِيَامِ بِهِ مِنَ المَنَافِعِ وَالمَصَالِحِ مَا لَا يُحْصَى، وَلَوْ لَمْ يَكُنْ فِيهِ إِلَّا أَنَّ هَذَا هُوَ الدِّينُ الَّذِي حَثَّ الشَّارِعُ عَلَيْهِ بِكُلِّ طَرِيقٍ وَأَعْظَمُ مَنْ يَلْزَمُهُ القِيَامُ بِهِ أَهْلُهُ، وَلِأَنَّهُ مِنْ أَعْظَمِ الأَدِلَّةِ عَلَى النُّصْحِ وَالإِخْلَاصِ اللَّذَيْنِ هُمَا قُطْبُ الدِّينِ وَرُوحُهُ، وَإِنَّ هَذَا الوَصْفَ

وَاعْلَمْ أَنَّ الْقَنَاعَةَ بِالْيَسِيرِ مِنَ الرِّزْقِ وَالِاقْتِصَادَ فِي أَمْرِ الْمَعِيشَةِ مَطْلُوبٌ مِنْ كُلِّ أَحَدٍ، لَا سِيَّمَا الْمُشْتَغِلُونَ بِالْعِلْمِ، فَإِنَّهُ كَالْمُتَعَيِّنِ عَلَيْهِمْ، لِأَنَّ الْعِلْمَ وَظِيفَةُ الْعُمْرِ كُلِّهِ أَوْ مُعْظَمِهِ، فَمَتَى زَاحَمَتْهُ الْأَشْغَالُ الدُّنْيَوِيَةُ وَالضَّرُورِيَاتُ حَصَلَ النَّقْصُ بِسَبَبِ ذَلِكَ، وَالِاقْتِصَادُ وَالْقَنَاعَةُ مِنْ أَكْبَرِ الْعَوَامِلِ لِحَصْرِ الْأَشْغَالِ الدُّنْيَوِيَةِ وَإِقْبَالُ الْمُتَعَلِّمِ عَلَى مَا هُوَ بِصَدَدِهِ.

وَمِنْ آدَابِ الْعَالِمِ وَالْمُتَعَلِّمِ النُّصْحُ وَبَثُّ الْعُلُومِ النَّافِعَةِ بِحَسَبِ الْإِمْكَانِ، حَتَّى لَوْ تَعَلَّمَ الْإِنْسَانُ مَسْأَلَةً وَبَثَّهَا كَانَ ذَلِكَ مِنْ بَرَكَةِ الْعِلْمِ، وَلِأَنَّ ثَمَرَاتِ الْعِلْمِ أَنْ يَأْخُذَهُ النَّاسُ عَنْكَ، فَمَنْ شَحَّ بِعِلْمِهِ مَاتَ عِلْمُهُ بِمَوْتِهِ، وَرُبَّمَا نَسِيَهُ وَهُوَ حَيٌّ، كَمَا أَنَّ مَنْ بَثَّ عِلْمَهُ كَانَ لَهُ حَيَاةٌ ثَانِيَةٌ وَحِفْظًا لِمَا عَلِمَهُ، وَجَزَاهُ اللَّهُ بِحَسَبِ عَمَلِهِ.

وَمِنْ أَهَمِّ مَا يَتَعَيَّنُ السَّعْيُ فِي جَمْعِ كَلِمَتِهِمْ وَتَأْلِيفُ الْقُلُوبِ عَلَى ذَلِكَ، وَحَسْمِ أَسْبَابِ الشَّرِّ وَالْعَدَاوَةِ وَالْبَغْضَاءِ بَيْنَهُمْ، وَأَنْ يَجْعَلُوا هَذَا الْأَمْرَ نُصْبَ أَعْيُنِهِمْ

آداب المعلمين والمتعلمين للإمام السعدي

مِنَ الِاشْتِغَالِ بِمَا يَنْفَعُهُمْ وَيَنْفَعُ النَّاسَ؛ وَهُوَ الِانْتِمَاءُ إِلَى مُعَلِّمِهِمْ، وَأَنَّهُمْ بِمَنْزِلَةِ أَوْلَادِهِ، وَحَقَّ نَفْعِ بَعْضِهِمْ بَعْضًا.

وَلِهَذَا يَنْبَغِي أَلَّا يَدَعَ مُمْكِنًا يَقْدِرُ عَلَيْهِ مِنْ نَفْعِ مَنْ يَقْدِرُ عَلَى نَفْعِهِ مِنْهُمْ مِنْ تَعْلِيمِهِ مَا يَجْهَلُ، وَالْبَحْثِ مَعَهُ لِلتَّعَاوُنِ عَلَى الْخَيْرِ وَإِرْشَادِهِ لِمَا فِيهِ نَفْعُهُ، وَيَنْبَغِي أَنْ يَكُونَ اجْتِمَاعُهُمْ فِي كُلِّ وَقْتٍ غَنِيمَةً يَتَعَلَّمُ فِيهِ الْقَاصِرُ مِمَّنْ هُوَ أَعْلَى مِنْهُ، وَيُعَلِّمُ الْعَارِفُ غَيْرَ الْعَارِفِ، وَيَتَطَارَحُونَ الْمَسَائِلَ النَّافِعَةَ، وَلْيَجْعَلُوا هَمَّهُمْ مَقْصُورًا عَلَى مَا هُمْ صَدَدِهِ، وَلْيَحْذَرُوا مِنَ الِاشْتِغَالِ بِالنَّاسِ وَالتَّفْتِيشِ عَنْ أَحْوَالِهِمْ وَالْعَيْبِ لَهُمْ، فَإِنَّهُ إِثْمٌ حَاضِرٌ.

وَالْمَعْصِيَةُ مِنْ أَهْلِ الْعِلْمِ أَعْظَمُ مِنْ غَيْرِهِمْ، لِأَنَّ الْحُجَّةَ عَلَيْهِمْ أَقْوَمُ، وَلِأَنَّ غَيْرَهُمْ يَقْتَدِي بِهِمْ، وَمَنْ كَانَ طَبْعُهُ الشَّرَّ مِنْ غَيْرِهِمْ جَعَلَهُمْ حُجَّةً لَهُ، وَلِأَنَّ الِاشْتِغَالَ بِالنَّاسِ يُضَيِّعُ الْمَصَالِحَ النَّافِعَةَ وَالْوَقْتَ النَّفِيسَ وَيُذْهِبُ بَهْجَةَ الْعِلْمِ وَنُورَهُ.

آداب المعلمين والمتعلمين للإمام السعدي

المُتَعَلِّمِينَ بِكُلِّ ما يَقْدِرُ عَلَيْهِ مِنَ التَّعْبِيرِ وَضَرْبِ الأَمْثَالِ وَالتَّصْوِيرِ وَالتَّحْرِيرِ، ثُمَّ لا يَنْتَقِلُ مِنْهَا إِلَى غَيْرِهَا قَبْلَ تَحَقُّقِهَا وَتَفْهِيمِهَا لِلْمُتَعَلِّمِينَ، وَلَا يَدَعُ المُتَعَلِّمِينَ يَخْرُجُونَ مِنَ المَوْضُوعِ الَّذِي لَمْ يَتِمَّ تَقْرِيرُهُ إِلَى مَوْضُوعٍ آخَرَ حَتَّى يُحْكِمُوهُ وَيَفْهَمُوهُ، فَإِنَّ الخُرُوجَ مِنَ المَوْضُوعِ إِلَى غَيْرِهِ قَبْلَ الِانْتِهَاءِ مِنْهُ يُشَوِّشُ الذِّهْنَ، وَيَحْرِمُ الفَائِدَةَ وَيَخْلِطُ المَسَائِلَ بَعْضَهَا بِبَعْضٍ.

وَيَنْبَغِي تَعَاهُدُ مَحْفُوظَاتِ المُتَعَلِّمِينَ وَمَعْلُومَاتِهِمْ بِالإِعَادَةِ وَالِامْتِحَانِ، وَالحَثِّ عَلَى المُذَاكَرَةِ وَالمُرَاجَعَةِ وَتَكْرَارِ الدَّرْسِ، فَإِنَّ التَّعَلُّمَ بِمَنْزِلَةِ الغَرْسِ لِلْأَشْجَارِ، وَالدَّرْسُ وَالمُذَاكَرَةُ وَالإِعَادَةُ بِمَنْزِلَةِ السَّقْيِ لَهَا وَإِزَالَةِ الأَشْيَاءِ المُضِرَّةِ لِتَنْمُوَ وَتَزْدَادَ عَلَى الدَّوَامِ.

وَكَمَا أَنَّ عَلَى المُتَعَلِّمِ تَوْقِيرَ مُعَلِّمِهِ وَالأَدَبَ مَعَهُ، فَكَذَلِكَ أَقْرَانُهُ فِي التَّعَلُّمِ مَعَهُ؛ عَلَيْهِ تَوْقِيرُهُمْ وَاحْتِرَامُهُمْ. فَالصُّحْبَةُ فِي طَلَبِ العِلْمِ تَجْمَعُ حُقُوقًا كَثِيرَةً؛ لِأَنَّ هُمْ حَقَّ الأُخُوَّةِ وَالصُّحْبَةِ، وَحَقَّ الِاحْتِرَامِ لِمَا قَامُوا بِهِ

وَمِنْ أَعْظَمِ مَا يَتَعَيَّنُ عَلَى أَهْلِ الْعِلْمِ الِاتِّصَافُ بِمَا يَدْعُو إِلَيْهِ الْعِلْمُ مِنَ الْأَخْلَاقِ وَالْأَعْمَالِ وَالتَّعْلِيمِ، فَهُمْ أَحَقُّ النَّاسِ بِالِاتِّصَافِ بِالْأَخْلَاقِ الْجَمِيلَةِ، وَالتَّخَلِّي مِنْ كُلِّ خُلُقٍ رَذِيلٍ، وَهُمْ أَوْلَى النَّاسِ بِالْقِيَامِ بِالْوَاجِبَاتِ الظَّاهِرَةِ وَالْبَاطِنَةِ وَتَرْكِ الْمُحَرَّمَاتِ، لِمَا تَمَيَّزُوا بِهِ مِنَ الْعِلْمِ وَالْمَعَارِفِ، الَّتِي لَمْ تَحْصُلْ لِغَيْرِهِمْ، وَلِأَنَّهُمْ قُدْوَةُ النَّاسِ فِي أُمُورِهِمْ وَلِأَنَّهُ يَتَطَرَّقُ إِلَيْهِمْ مِنَ الِاعْتِرَاضِ وَالْقَوَادِحِ عِنْدَمَا يَتْرُكُونَ مَا يَدْعُو إِلَيْهِ الْعِلْمُ أَعْظَمُ مِمَّا يَتَطَرَّقُ إِلَى غَيْرِهِمْ.

وَأَيْضًا فَكَانَ السَّلَفُ يَسْتَعِينُونَ بِالْعَمَلِ عَلَى الْعِلْمِ؛ فَإِنْ عُمِلَ بِهِ اسْتَقَرَّ وَدَامَ وَكَثُرَتْ بَرَكَتُهُ، وَإِنْ تُرِكَ الْعَمَلُ بِهِ ذَهَبَ أَوْ عُدِمَتْ بَرَكَتُهُ، فَرُوحُ الْعِلْمِ وَحَيَاتُهُ وَقَوَامُهُ إِنَّمَا هُوَ بِالْقِيَامِ بِهِ عَمَلًا وَتَخَلُّقًا وَتَعْلِيمًا وَنُصْحًا، وَلَا حَوْلَ وَلَا قُوَّةَ إِلَّا بِاللهِ.

وَيَنْبَغِي سُلُوكُ الطَّرِيقِ النَّافِعِ عِنْدَ الْبَحْثِ تَعَلُّمًا وَتَعْلِيمًا، فَإِذَا شَرَعَ الْمُعَلِّمُ فِي مَسْأَلَةٍ وَضَّحَهَا وَأَوْصَلَهَا إِلَى أَفْهَامِ

فَإِنَّهُ إِذَا جَعَلَ هَذَا الْأَمْرَ نَصْبَ عَيْنَيْهِ وَأَعْيُنِهِمْ تَنَوَّرَتِ الْأَفْكَارُ، وَعُرِفَتِ الْمَآخِذُ وَالْبَرَاهِينُ، وَاتُّبِعَتِ الْحَقَائِقُ، وَكَانَ الْقَصْدُ الْأَصْلِيُّ وَتَوَابِعُهُ مَعْرِفَةَ الْحَقِّ وَاتِّبَاعَهُ.

وَالْحَذَرَ الْحَذَرَ مِنَ التَّعَصُّبِ لِلْأَقْوَالِ وَالْقَائِلِينَ؛ وَهُوَ أَنْ يَجْعَلَ الْقَصْدَ مِنَ الْمُنَاظَرَةِ نَصْرَ الْقَوْلِ الَّذِي قَالَهُ أَوْ قَالَهُ مَنْ يُعَظِّمُهُ، فَإِنَّ التَّعَصُّبَ مُذْهِبٌ لِلْإِخْلَاصِ، مُزِيلٌ لِبَهْجَةِ الْعِلْمِ، مُعْمٍ لِلْحَقَائِقِ، فَاتِحٌ لِأَبْوَابِ الْخِصَامِ وَالْحِقْدِ، كَمَا أَنَّ الْإِنْصَافَ هُوَ زِينَةُ الْعِلْمِ، وَعُنْوَانُ الْإِخْلَاصِ وَالنُّصْحِ وَالْفَلَاحِ.

وَلْيَحْذَرْ مِنْ طَلَبِ الْعِلْمِ لِلْأَغْرَاضِ الْفَاسِدَةِ وَالْمَقَاصِدِ السَّيِّئَةِ؛ مِنَ الْمُبَاهَاةِ وَالْمُمَارَاةِ وَالرِّيَاءِ وَالسُّمْعَةِ، أَوْ أَنْ يَكُونَ لَهُ وَسِيلَةً إِلَى الْأَغْرَاضِ الدُّنْيَوِيَّةِ وَالرِّئَاسَةِ، فَلَيْسَتْ هَذِهِ حَالَ أَهْلِ الْعِلْمِ الَّذِينَ هُمْ أَهْلُهُ فِي الْحَقِيقَةِ، وَمَنْ طَلَبَ الْعِلْمَ وَاسْتَعْمَلَهُ فِي أَغْرَاضِهِ السَّيِّئَةِ أَوْ رِيَاءً أَوْ سُمْعَةً فَلَيْسَ لَهُ فِي الْآخِرَةِ مِنْ خَلَاقٍ.

وَمِنْهَا: أَنَّهُ إِذَا تَوَقَّفَ وَقَالَ: اللهُ أَعْلَمُ. فَمَا أَسْرَعَ أَنْ يَأْتِيَهُ عِلْمُ ذَلِكَ، إِمَّا مِنْ مُرَاجَعَتِهِ أَوْ مُرَاجَعَةِ غَيْرِهِ، فَإِنَّ المُتَعَلِّمَ إِذَا رَأَى مُعَلِّمَهُ جَدَّ وَاجْتَهَدَ فِي تَحْصِيلِ عِلْمِهَا وَإِتْحَافِ المُعَلِّمِ بِهَا، فَمَا أَحْسَنَ هَذَا الأَثَرَ.

وَمِنْهَا: أَنَّهُ إِذَا تَوَقَّفَ عَمَّا لَا يَعْرِفُ كَانَ دَلِيلًا عَلَى ثِقَتِهِ وَإِتْقَانِهِ فِيمَا يَجْزِمُ بِهِ مِنَ المَسَائِلِ، كَمَا أَنَّ مَنْ عُرِفَ مِنْهُ الإِقْدَامُ عَلَى الكَلَامِ فِيمَا لَا يَعْلَمُ؛ كَانَ ذَلِكَ دَاعِيًا لِلرَّيْبِ فِي كُلِّ مَا يَتَكَلَّمُ بِهِ، حَتَّى فِي الأُمُورِ الوَاضِحَةِ.

وَمِنْهَا: أَنَّ المُعَلِّمَ إِذَا رَأَى مِنْهُ المُتَعَلِّمُونَ تَوَقُّفَهُ عَمَّا لَا يَعْلَمُ؛ كَانَ ذَلِكَ تَعْلِيمًا لَهُمْ وَإِرْشَادًا إِلَى هَذِهِ الطَّرِيقَةِ الحَسَنَةِ، وَالاِقْتِدَاءُ بِالأَحْوَالِ وَالأَعْمَالِ أَبْلَغُ مِنَ الاِقْتِدَاءِ بِالأَقْوَالِ.

وَمِمَّا يُعِينُ عَلَى هَذَا المَطْلُوبِ أَنْ يَفْتَحَ المُعَلِّمُ لِلْمُتَعَلِّمِينَ بَابَ المُنَاظَرَةِ فِي المَسَائِلِ وَالاِحْتِجَاجِ عَلَيْهَا، وَأَنْ يَكُونَ القَصْدُ وَاحِدًا، وَهُوَ اتِّبَاعُ مَا رَجَّحَتْهُ الحُجَّةُ وَالأَدِلَّةُ،

وَكَمَا أَنَّ هَذَا لَازِمٌ عَلَى المُتَعَلِّمِ، فَعَلَى المُعَلِّمِ إِذَا أَخْطَأَ أَنْ يَرْجِعَ إِلَى الحَقِّ، وَلَا يَمْنَعُهُ قَوْلٌ قَالَهُ ثُمَّ رَأَى الحَقَّ فِي خِلَافِهِ مِنْ مُرَاجَعَةِ الحَقِّ وَالرُّجُوعِ إِلَيْهِ، فَإِنَّ هَذَا عَلَامَةُ الإِنْصَافِ وَالتَّوَاضُعِ لِلْحَقِّ، فَالوَاجِبُ اتِّبَاعُ الصَّوَابِ سَوَاءٌ جَاءَ عَلَى يَدِ الصَّغِيرِ أَوِ الكَبِيرِ.

وَمِنْ نِعْمَةِ اللهِ عَلَى المُعَلِّمِ أَنْ يَجِدَ مِنْ تَلَامِيذِهِ مَنْ يُنَبِّهَهُ عَلَى خَطَئِهِ وَيُرْشِدَهُ إِلَى الصَّوَابِ، وَيَزُولَ اسْتِمْرَارُهُ عَلَى جَهْلِهِ، فَهَذَا يَحْتَاجُ إِلَى شُكْرِ اللهِ ثُمَّ إِلَى شُكْرِ مَنْ أَجْرَى اللهُ الهُدَى عَلَى يَدَيْهِ مُتَعَلِّمًا أَوْ غَيْرَهُ.

وَمِنْ أَعْظَمِ مَا يَجِبُ لِلْمُعَلِّمِينَ أَنْ يَقُولُوا لِمَا لَا يَعْلَمُونَهُ: اللهُ أَعْلَمُ، وَلَيْسَ هَذَا بِنَاقِصٍ لِأَقْدَارِهِمْ، بَلْ هَذَا مِمَّا يَزِيدُ قَدْرَهُمْ، وَيُسْتَدَلُّ بِهِ عَلَى دِينِهِمْ وَتَحَرِّيهِمْ لِلصَّوَابِ.

وَفِي تَوَقُّفِهِ عَمَّا لَا يَعْلَمُهُ فَوَائِدُ كَثِيرَةٌ:

مِنْهَا: أَنَّ هَذَا هُوَ الوَاجِبُ عَلَيْهِ.

آداب المعلمين والمتعلمين للإمام السعدي

وَلَا يَخْرُجُ عَنْ إِشَارَتِهِ وَإِرْشَادِهِ، وَلْيَجْلِسْ بَيْنَ يَدَيْهِ مُتَأَدِّبًا، وَيُظْهِرُ غَايَةَ حَاجَتِهِ إِلَى عِلْمِهِ، وَيَدْعُو لَهُ حَاضِرًا وَغَائِبًا، وَإِذَا أَتْحَفَهُ بِفَائِدَةٍ وَتَوْضِيحٍ لِعِلْمٍ فَلَا يُظْهِرُ لَهُ أَنَّهُ قَدْ عَرَفَهُ قَبْلَ ذَلِكَ وَإِنْ كَانَ عَارِفًا لَهُ، بَلْ يُصْغِي إِلَيْهِ إِصْغَاءَ الْمُتَطَلِّبِ بِشِدَّةٍ إِلَى الْفَائِدَةِ، هَذَا فِيمَا يَعْرِفُهُ؟! فَكَيْفَ بِمَا لَا يَعْرِفُهُ؟ وَلِهَذَا كَانَ هَذَا الْأَدَبُ مُسْتَحْسَنًا مَعَ كُلِّ أَحَدٍ فِي الْعُلُومِ وَالْمُخَاطَبَاتِ وَفِي الْأُمُورِ الدِّينِيَّةِ وَالدُّنْيَوِيَّةِ.

وَإِذَا أَخْطَأَ الْمُعَلِّمُ فِي شَيْءٍ فَلْيُنَبِّهْهُ بِرِفْقٍ وَلُطْفٍ بِحَسْبِ الْمَقَامِ، وَلَا يَقُولُ لَهُ: أَخْطَأْتَ، أَوْ لَيْسَ الْأَمْرُ كَمَا تَقُولُ، بَلْ يَأْتِي بِعِبَارَةٍ لَطِيفَةٍ يُدْرِكُ بِهَا الْمُعَلِّمُ خَطَأَهُ مِنْ دُونِ أَنْ يَتَشَوَّشَ قَلْبُهُ، فَإِنَّ هَذَا مِنَ الْحُقُوقِ اللَّازِمَةِ، وَهُوَ أَدْعَى لِلْوُصُولِ إِلَى الصَّوَابِ، فَإِنَّ الرَّدَّ الَّذِي يَصْحَبُهُ سُوءُ الْأَدَبِ، وَانْزِعَاجُ الْقَلْبِ يَمْنَعُ مِنْ تَصَوُّرِ الصَّوَابِ مِنْ قَصْدِهِ.

وَالبَلَدُ الَّذِي لَيْسَ فِيهِ مَنْ يُبَيِّنُ لِلنَّاسِ أَمْرَ دِينِهِمْ وَيُرْشِدُهُمْ لِمَا يَنْتَابُهُمْ مِمَّا هُمْ مُضْطَرُّونَ إِلَيْهِ، لَا خَيْرَ فِي الإِقَامَةِ فِيهِ. فَمَنْ هَذَا إِحْسَانُهُ وَأَثَرُهُ كَيْفَ لَا يَجِبُ عَلَى كُلِّ مُسْلِمٍ مَحَبَّتُهُ وَتَوْقِيرُهُ وَالقِيَامُ بِحُقُوقِهِ؟

وَأَمَّا حَقُّهُ الخَاصُّ عَلَى المُتَعَلِّمِ فَلِمَا بَذَلَهُ مِنْ تَعْلِيمِهِ، وَالحِرْصِ عَلَى مَا يُرْشِدُهُ وَيُوصِلُهُ إِلَى أَعْلَى الدَّرَجَاتِ، فَلَيْسَ نَفْعُ الآبَاءِ وَالأُمَّهَاتِ نَظِيرًا لِنَفْعِ المُعَلِّمِينَ المُرَبِّينَ لِلنَّاسِ بِصِغَارِ العِلْمِ قَبْلَ كِبَارِهِ، البَاذِلِينَ نَفَائِسَ أَوْقَاتِهِمْ وَصَفْوَةَ أَفْكَارِهِمْ فِي تَفْهِيمِ المُسْتَرْشِدِينَ بِكُلِّ طَرِيقٍ وَوَسِيلَةٍ يَقْدِرُونَ عَلَيْهَا، وَإِذَا كَانَ مَنْ أَحْسَنَ إِلَى الإِنْسَانِ بِهَدِيَّةٍ مَالِيَّةٍ يَنْتَفِعُ بِهَا، ثُمَّ تَذْهَبُ وَتَزُولُ، لَهُ حَقٌّ كَبِيرٌ عَلَى المُحْسَنِ إِلَيْهِ، فَمَا الظَّنُّ بِهَدَايَا العِلْمِ النَّافِعِ الكَثِيرَةِ المُتَنَوِّعَةِ؛ البَاقِي نَفْعُهَا مَا دَامَ العَبْدُ حَيًّا وَبَعْدَ مَمَاتِهِ المُتَسَلْسِلُ بِحَسْبِ حَالِ تِلْكَ الهَدَايَا، فَحِينَئِذٍ يَعْرِفُ حَقَّهُ وَيُوَقِّرُهُ وَيُحْسِنُ الأَدَبَ مَعَهُ.

آداب المعلمين والمتعلمين للإمام السعدي

وَلْيُرَغِّبِ الْمُتَعَلِّمَ بِكُلِّ طَرِيقٍ وَلَا يُمِلَّهُ بِاشْتِغَالِهِ بِمَا يَعْسُرُ عَلَى فَهْمِهِ مِنْ أَنْوَاعِ الْعُلُومِ وَمُفْرَدَاتِهَا.

وَعَلَى الْمُتَعَلِّمِ أَنْ يُوَقِّرَ مُعَلِّمَهُ وَيَتَأَدَّبَ مَعَهُ حَسْبَ مَا يَقْدِرُ عَلَيْهِ لِمَا لَهُ مِنَ الْحَقِّ الْعَامِّ وَالْخَاصِّ:

أَمَّا الْعَامُّ فَإِنَّ مُعَلِّمَ الْخَيْرِ قَدِ اسْتَعَدَّ لِنَفْعِ الْخَلْقِ بِتَعْلِيمِهِ وَفَتْوَاهُ، فَحَقُّهُ عَلَى النَّاسِ حَقُّ الْمُحْسِنِينَ، وَلَا إِحْسَانَ أَعْظَمَ وَأَنْفَعَ مِنْ إِحْسَانِ مَنْ يُرْشِدُ النَّاسَ لِأَمْرِ دِينِهِمْ، وَيُعَلِّمُهُمْ مَا جَهِلُوا وَيُنَبِّهُهُمْ لِمَا غَفَلُوا، وَيَحْصُلُ بِسَبَبِ ذَلِكَ مِنَ الْخَيْرِ، وَانْقِمَاعِ الشَّرِّ وَنَشْرِ الدِّينِ وَالْمَعَارِفِ النَّافِعَةِ، مَا هُوَ أَنْفَعُ شَيْءٍ لِلْمَوْجُودِينَ وَمَنْ أَتَى مِنْ بَعْدِهِمْ مِنْ ذُرِّيَّتِهِمْ وَغَيْرِهِمْ.

فَلَوْلَا الْعِلْمُ كَانَ النَّاسُ كَالْبَهَائِمِ فِي ظُلْمَةٍ يَتَخَبَّطُونَ، وَفِي غَيِّهِمْ يَعْمَهُونَ، فَهُوَ النُّورُ الَّذِي يُهْتَدَى بِهِ فِي الظُّلُمَاتِ، وَالْحَيَاةُ لِلْقُلُوبِ وَالْأَرْوَاحِ وَالدِّينِ وَالدُّنْيَا.

غَيرِهِ، وَحَيثُ كَانَ مَا يَحمِلُهُ مِنَ العِلمِ هُوَ عَينُ بِضَاعَةِ المُعَلِّمِ يَحفَظُهَا وَيُنَمِّيهَا، وَيَطلُبُ بِهَا المَكَاسِبَ الرَّابِحَةَ، فَهُوَ الوَلَدُ الحَقِيقِيُّ لِلمُعَلِّمِ الوَارِثُ لَهُ، قَالَ تَعَالَى: ﴿فَهَبْ لِى مِن لَّدُنكَ وَلِيًّا ۝ يَرِثُنِى وَيَرِثُ مِنْ ءَالِ يَعْقُوبَ﴾ [مَريَـم:٥-٦].

وَالمُرَادُ وِرَاثَةُ العِلمِ وَالحِكمَةِ، فَالمُعَلِّمُ مُثَابٌ مَأجُورٌ عَلَى نَفسِ تَعلِيمِهِ، سَوَاءٌ فَهِمَ أَو لَم يَفهَم، فَإِذَا فَهِمَ مَا عَلِمَهُ وَانتَفَعَ بِهِ بِنَفسِهِ وَنَفَعَ غَيرَهُ كَانَ أَجرًا جَارِيًا لِلمُعَلِّمِ مَا دَامَ ذَلِكَ النَّفعُ مُتَسَلسِلًا مُتَّصِلًا، وَهَذِهِ تِجَارَةٌ بِمِثلِهَا يَتَنَافَسُ المُوَفَّقُونَ، فَعَلَى المُعَلِّمِ أَن يَسعَى سَعيًا شَدِيدًا فِي إِيجَادِ هَذِهِ التِّجَارَةِ وَتَنمِيَتِهَا، فَهِيَ مِن عَمَلِهِ وَآثَارِ عَمَلِهِ، قَالَ تَعَالَى: ﴿إِنَّا نَحْنُ نُحْىِ ٱلْمَوْتَىٰ وَنَكْتُبُ مَا قَدَّمُوا۟ وَءَاثَـٰرَهُمْ﴾ [يـس:١٢]. فَ ﴿مَا قَدَّمُوا۟﴾: مَا بَاشَرُوا عَمَلَهُ، ﴿وَءَاثَـٰرَهُمْ﴾: مَا تَرَتَّبَ عَلَى أَعمَالِهِم مِنَ المَصَالِحِ وَالمَنَافِعِ أَو ضِدِّهَا.

فَإِنَّ هَذَا مِنْ عَدَمِ النُّصْحِ، فَإِنَّ القَلِيلَ الَّذِي يَفْهَمُهُ وَيَعْقِلُهُ خَيْرٌ مِنَ الْكَثِيرِ الَّذِي هُوَ عُرْضَةٌ لِعَدَمِ الفَهْمِ وَالنِّسْيَانِ، وَكَذَلِكَ يُلْقِي إِلَيْهِ مِنَ التَّوْضِيحِ وَالتَّقْرِيرِ لِدَرْسِهِ بِقَدْرِ مَا يَتَّسِعُ فَهْمُهُ لِإِدْرَاكِهِ، وَلَا يَخْلِطُ المَسَائِلَ بَعْضَهَا بِبَعْضٍ، وَلَا يَنْتَقِلُ مِنْ نَوْعٍ مِنْ أَنْوَاعِ المَسَائِلِ إِلَى نَوْعٍ آخَرَ حَتَّى يَتَصَوَّرَ وَيُحَقِّقَ السَّابِقَ؛ فَإِنَّهُ دَرْكٌ لِلسَّابِقِ وَلِيَتَوَفَّرَ فَهْمُهُ عَلَى اللَّاحِقِ.

فَأَمَّا إِذَا أَدْخَلَ المَسَائِلَ بَعْضَهَا بِبَعْضٍ قَبْلَ فَهْمِ المُتَعَلِّمِ فَإِنَّهُ سَبَبٌ لِإِضَاعَةِ الأَوَّلِ وَعَدَمِ فَهْمِ اللَّاحِقِ، ثُمَّ تَتَزَاحَمُ عَلَيْهِ المَسَائِلُ الَّتِي لَمْ يَتَحَقَّقْهَا فَيَمَلُّهَا وَيَضِيقُ عَطَنُهُ عَنِ العَوْدِ عَلَيْهَا، فَلَا يَنْبَغِي أَنْ يُهْمِلَ هَذَا الأَمْرَ.

وَعَلَى المُعَلِّمِ النُّصْحُ لِلْمُتَعَلِّمِ بِكُلِّ مَا يَقْدِرُ عَلَيْهِ مِنَ التَّعْلِيمِ وَالصَّبْرِ عَلَى عَدَمِ إِدْرَاكِهِ، وَعَلَى عَدَمِ أَدَبِهِ وَجَفَائِهِ، مَعَ شِدَّةِ حِرْصِهِ عَلَى مَا يَقَوِّمُهُ وَيُحَسِّنُ أَدَبَهُ، لِأَنَّ المُتَعَلِّمَ لَهُ حَقٌّ عَلَى المُعَلِّمِ حَيْثُ أَقْبَلَ عَلَى العِلْمِ الَّذِي يَنْفَعُهُ وَيَنْفَعُ النَّاسَ، وَحَيْثُ تَوَجَّهَ لِلْمُعَلِّمِ دُونَ

كَرَامَتِهِ، وَلِيَتَحَقَّقُوا بِقَوْلِهِ صَلَّى اللهُ عَلَيْهِ وَسَلَّمَ: «مَنْ سَلَكَ طَرِيقاً يَلْتَمِسُ فِيهِ عِلْماً سَهَّلَ اللهُ لَهُ طَرِيقاً إِلَى الجَنَّةِ».

فَكُلُّ طَرِيقٍ حِسِّيٍّ أَوْ مَعْنَوِيٍّ يَسْلُكُهُ أَهْلُ العِلْمِ يُعِينُ عَلَى العِلْمِ أَوْ يُحَصِّلُهُ؛ فَإِنَّهُ دَاخِلٌ فِي هَذَا.

ثُمَّ بَعْدَ هَذَا فَيَتَعَيَّنُ البُدَاءَةُ بِالأَهَمِّ فَالأَهَمِّ مِنَ العُلُومِ الشَّرْعِيَّةِ، وَمَا يُعِينُ عَلَيْهَا مِنْ عُلُومِ العَرَبِيَّةِ، وَتَفْصِيلُ هَذِهِ الجُمْلَةِ مَعْرُوفٌ، وَيَنْبَغِي أَنْ يَسْلُكَ أَقْرَبَ طَرِيقٍ يُوصِلُ إِلَى المَطْلُوبِ الَّذِي قَصَدَهُ، وَأَنْ يَنْتَقِيَ مِنْ مُصَنَّفَاتِ الفَنِّ الَّذِي يَشْتَغِلُ فِيهِ أَحْسَنَهَا وَأَوْضَحَهَا وَأَكْثَرَهَا فَائِدَةً، وَيَجْعَلَ جُلَّ هَمِّهِ وَاشْتِغَالِهِ بِذَلِكَ الكِتَابِ حِفْظًا عِنْدَ الإِمْكَانِ، أَوْ دِرَاسَةَ تَكْرِيرٍ، بِحَيْثُ تَكُونُ المَعَانِي مَعْقُولَةً لَهُ مَحْفُوظَةً، ثُمَّ لَا يَزَالُ يُكَرِّرُ مَا مَرَّ عَلَيْهِ وَيُعِيدُهُ.

وَعَلَى المُعَلِّمِ أَنْ يَنْظُرَ إِلَى ذِهْنِ المُتَعَلِّمِ وَقُوَّةِ اسْتِعْدَادِهِ أَوْ ضَعْفِهِ، فَلَا يَدَعُهُ يَشْتَغِلُ بِكِتَابٍ لَا يُنَاسِبُ حَالَهُ؛

آداب المعلمين والمتعلمين للإمام السعدي

المَتْنُ: فَائِدَةٌ تَشْتَمِلُ عَلَى نُبْذَةٍ مِنْ آدَابِ المُعَلِّمِينَ وَالمُتَعَلِّمِينَ

بِسْمِ اللهِ الرَّحْمَنِ الرَّحِيمِ

يَتَعَيَّنُ عَلَى أَهْلِ العِلْمِ مِنَ المُعَلِّمِينَ وَالمُتَعَلِّمِينَ أَنْ يَجْعَلُوا أَسَاسَ أَمْرِهِمْ؛ الَّذِي يَبْنُونَ عَلَيْهِ حَرَكَاتِهِمْ وَسَكَنَاتِهِمْ الإِخْلَاصَ الكَامِلَ وَالتَّقَرُّبَ إِلَى اللهِ بِهَذِهِ العِبَادَةِ، التِي هِيَ مِنْ أَجَلِّ العِبَادَاتِ وَأَكْمَلِهَا وَأَنْفَعِهَا وَأَعَمِّهَا، وَيَتَفَقَّدُوا هَذَا الأَصْلَ الجَلِيلَ فِي كُلِّ دَقِيقٍ مِنْ أَمْرِهِمْ وَجَلِيلٍ.

فَإِنْ دَرَسُوا أَوْ دَارَسُوا، أَوْ بَحَثُوا أَوْ نَاظَرُوا، أَوْ أَسْمَعُوا أَوِ اسْتَمَعُوا، أَوْ كَتَبُوا أَوْ حَفِظُوا، أَوْ كَرَّرُوا دُرُوسَهُمُ الخَاصَّةَ، أَوْ رَاجَعُوا عَلَيْهَا أَوْ عَلَى غَيْرِهَا مِنَ الكُتُبِ الأُخْرَى، أَوْ جَلَسُوا لِمَجْلِسِ عِلْمٍ، أَوْ نَقَلُوا أَقْدَامَهُمْ لِمَجَالِسِ العِلْمِ، أَوِ اشْتَرَوْا كُتُبًا أَوْ مَا يُعِينُ عَلَى العِلْمِ، كَانَ الإِخْلَاصُ لِلهِ وَاحْتِسَابُ أَجْرِهِ وَثَوَابِهِ مُلَازِمًا لَهُمْ، لِيَصِيرَ اشْتِغَالُهُمْ كُلُّهُ قُرْبَةً وَطَاعَةً وَسَيْرًا إِلَى اللهِ وَإِلَى

من آداب المعلمين والمتعلمين

تأليف
الشيخ العلامة
عبد الرحمن بن ناصر السعدي
رحمه الله تعالى

Who are we?

Lum'ah al-Lughah is an Arabic language learning institute dedicated to opening the door of the Arabic language to English-speaking audiences. Our mission is not merely linguistic, but rooted in clarity, authenticity, and a sincere commitment to the sources of Islām.

We follow the path of the Book and Sunnah upon the understanding of the pious predecessors, ensuring that the knowledge we impart is firmly grounded in the pure methodology of the early generations of Islām. Our approach is shaped by the guidance of the scholars of this era — among them Shaykhs Ibn Bāz, Al-Albānī, Ibn al-'Uthaymīn, Ṣāliḥ al-Fawzān, Muqbil, Rabee', 'Ubayd al-Jābirī, and others. May Allāh have mercy upon those who have passed away and preserve those who remain.

At Lum'ah al-Lughah, under the guidance of our head tutor Khālid Abū Zayd, who has over 30 years of experience teaching Arabic to English-speaking students — we see Arabic, just as the scholars have mentioned, as the key to understanding the Qur'ān, the Sunnah, and the words of the scholars with precision. Our work is built on sound methodology, precision, and dedication to providing our students with both the language tools and the Islamic framework needed to connect to authentic knowledge.

www.ingramcontent.com/pod-product-compliance
Lightning Source LLC
Chambersburg PA
CBHW031418040426
42444CB00005B/628